YOU CAN DRAW IT!

BIG CATS

WRITTEN BY JON EPPARD
ILLUSTRATED BY STEVE PORTER

BELLWETHER MEDIA · MINNEAPOLIS, MN

This edition first published in 2013 by Bellwether Media, Inc.

Library of Congress Cataloging-in-Publication Data

Eppard, Jon.
  Big cats / by Jon Eppard.
      pages cm – (You can draw it!)
  Includes bibliographical references and index.
  Summary: "Information accompanies step-by-step instructions on how to draw big cats. The text level and subject
matter is intended for students in grades 3 through 7"–Provided by publisher.
  ISBN 978-1-60014-809-5 (hardcover : alk. paper) – ISBN 978-1-60014-854-5 (pbk. : alk. paper)
  1. Felidae in art–Juvenile literature. 2. Drawing–Technique–Juvenile literature. I. Title.
  NC783.8.F45E67 2012
  743.6'975–dc23
                          2012018180

Printed in the United States of America, North Mankato, MN.

TABLE OF CONTENTS

BIG CATS!

Big cats are large, aggressive members of the **feline** family. With beautiful fur coats, they are dressed to kill. These wild cats are also born to hunt. They silently stalk, chase, and ambush prey. Then they **suffocate** captured animals with a deadly bite to the throat. Big cats have both the beauty and the strength to take your breath away!

DRAWING FROM PHOTOS IS A GREAT PLACE TO START. WORK YOUR WAY UP TO DRAWING FROM MEMORY OR YOUR IMAGINATION.

Before you begin drawing, you will need a few basic supplies.

PAPER

DRAWING PENCILS

BLACK INK PEN

2B OR NOT 2B?

NOT ALL DRAWING PENCILS ARE THE SAME. "B" PENCILS ARE SOFTER, MAKE DARKER MARKS, AND SMUDGE EASILY. "H" PENCILS ARE HARDER, MAKE LIGHTER MARKS, AND DON'T SMUDGE VERY MUCH AT ALL.

COLORED PENCILS
(ALL DRAWINGS IN THIS BOOK WERE FINISHED WITH COLORED PENCILS.)

ERASER

PENCIL SHARPENER

Bobcat
The Lynx Look-Alike

The bobcat shares many physical features with the lynx, another big cat. It is easy for the bobcat to pose as the lynx. However, look beyond the beard and **tufts** of hair on the ears. The bobcat has shorter legs and a darker coat. It also has a white tip on its **bobbed** tail.

1

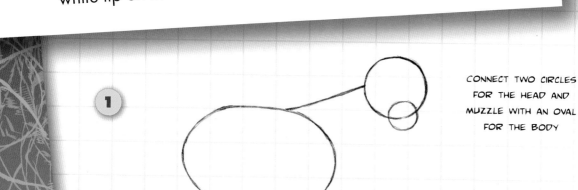

CONNECT TWO CIRCLES FOR THE HEAD AND MUZZLE WITH AN OVAL FOR THE BODY

BREAK IT DOWN

JUST ABOUT ANY SUBJECT YOU'RE DRAWING CAN BE BROKEN DOWN INTO SMALLER PARTS. LOOK FOR CIRCLES, OVALS, SQUARES, AND OTHER BASIC SHAPES THAT CAN HELP BUILD YOUR DRAWING.

2

ADD THE LEGS AND POINTED EARS

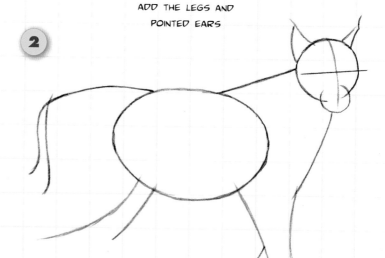

DRAW THE OUTLINE OF THE
PAWS, TAIL, AND BEARD

3

4

ADD SPOTS, HAIR, AND
FACIAL DETAILS

INK AND COLOR

THE BOBCAT CAN VARY IN
COLOR FROM YELLOWISH TO
REDDISH BROWN. LEAVE THE
UNDERSIDE AND AREA AROUND
THE MOUTH WHITE.

5

Mountain Lion
The Cat with Many Names

The mountain lion goes by many names. Cougar, puma, and catamount are all **aliases**. The mountain lion's **elusive** nature has also earned it the nicknames "ghost cat" and "shadow cat." Although this cat is most often in hiding, it sometimes emerges for a fierce fight!

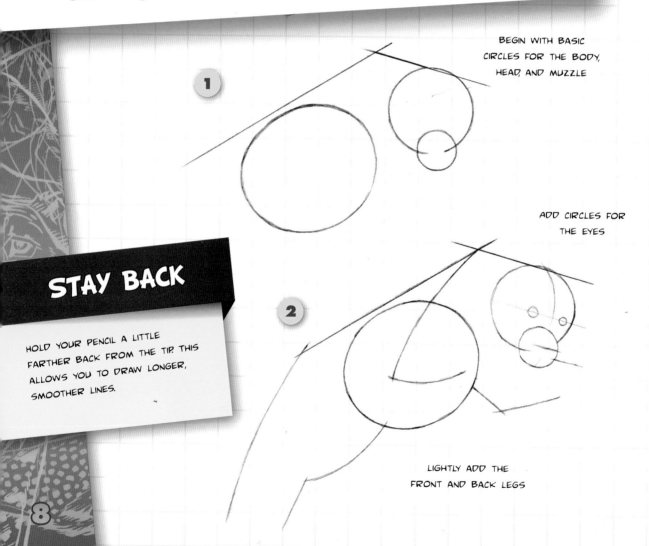

1

BEGIN WITH BASIC CIRCLES FOR THE BODY, HEAD, AND MUZZLE

ADD CIRCLES FOR THE EYES

2

LIGHTLY ADD THE FRONT AND BACK LEGS

STAY BACK

HOLD YOUR PENCIL A LITTLE FARTHER BACK FROM THE TIP. THIS ALLOWS YOU TO DRAW LONGER, SMOOTHER LINES.

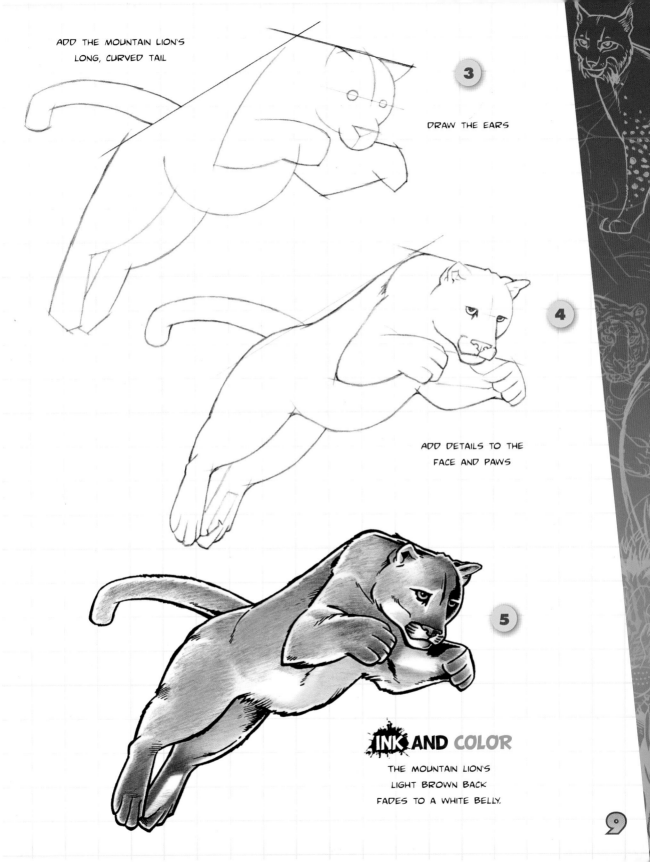

ADD THE MOUNTAIN LION'S
LONG, CURVED TAIL

3

DRAW THE EARS

4

ADD DETAILS TO THE
FACE AND PAWS

5

INK AND COLOR

THE MOUNTAIN LION'S
LIGHT BROWN BACK
FADES TO A WHITE BELLY.

9

Cheetah
The Fastest Land Mammal

The cheetah regularly takes part in high-speed chases. It either catches up to its prey or goes hungry. The cat has been clocked at speeds over 60 miles (97 kilometers) per hour! Though it uses its speed in short bursts, the cheetah is still exhausted after a hunt. It must catch its breath and cool down before it can feast.

SMUDGE IT

SMUDGING YOUR PENCIL MARKS WITH A WET FINGER OR SMUDGE STICK WILL GIVE YOU A VARIETY OF GRAY TONES.

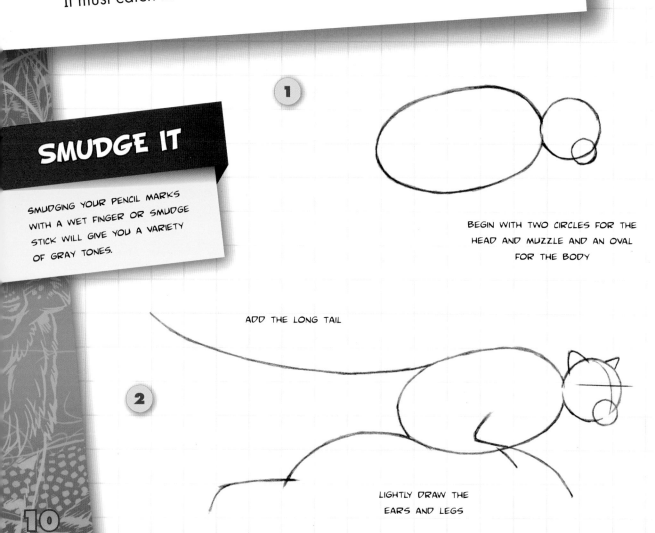

1

BEGIN WITH TWO CIRCLES FOR THE HEAD AND MUZZLE AND AN OVAL FOR THE BODY

ADD THE LONG TAIL

2

LIGHTLY DRAW THE EARS AND LEGS

COMPLETE THE OUTLINE
OF THE TAIL AND LEGS

3

DON'T FORGET THE
BLACK LINES BELOW
THE EYES

4

ADD SPOTS AND
OTHER DETAILS

5

INK AND COLOR

CHEETAHS ARE YELLOWISH TAN
WITH A WHITE UNDERSIDE.

11

Caracal
The Bird Hunter

The house cat gets the mouse, but the caracal gets the bird! Its 10-foot (3-meter) vertical leap lets it grab birds out of the air. Its sharp claws help it climb trees and snatch birds from branches. Even the fastest bird on land, the ostrich, cannot outrun the caracal!

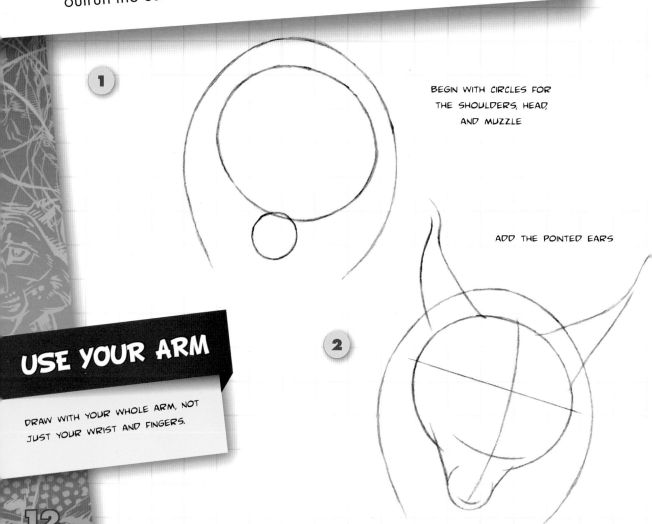

1

BEGIN WITH CIRCLES FOR THE SHOULDERS, HEAD, AND MUZZLE

ADD THE POINTED EARS

2

USE YOUR ARM

DRAW WITH YOUR WHOLE ARM, NOT JUST YOUR WRIST AND FINGERS.

DRAW THE SLANTED EYES
AND SHARP TEETH

3

ADD THE WHISKERS AND
OTHER FACIAL DETAILS

4

5

INK AND COLOR

CARACALS ARE TAN AND BROWN
WITH WHITE AROUND THE MOUTH.

13

Leopard
The Master of Camouflage

The leopard is a master of **camouflage**. In dry grasslands, it sports a tan coat. In rain forests, it wears black. Whether its coat is light or dark in color, it is always polka-dotted. You will never spot this cat without its signature **rosettes**.

LIGHT TO DARK

BEGIN YOUR DRAWING WITH VERY LIGHT LINES. SLOWLY BUILD UP TO DARK LINES AS YOU REACH THE FINAL STEPS. THIS WILL ALLOW FOR EASY CORRECTION OF MISTAKES.

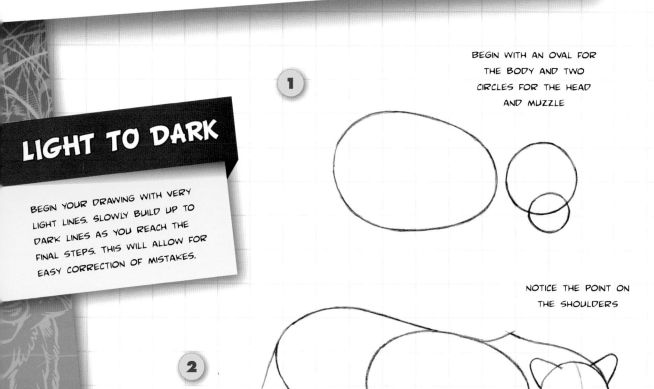

BEGIN WITH AN OVAL FOR THE BODY AND TWO CIRCLES FOR THE HEAD AND MUZZLE

NOTICE THE POINT ON THE SHOULDERS

LIGHTLY ADD THE TAIL, LEGS, AND EARS

ADD THE EYES

3

COMPLETE THE OUTLINE
OF THE PAWS AND TAIL

4

ADD THE ROSETTES
AND WHISKERS

5

INK AND COLOR

THIS LEOPARD IS YELLOWISH TAN WITH
A WHITE UNDERBELLY. FADED ORANGE
SPOTS ARE INSIDE THE ROSETTES.

15

Lion
The Most Prideful Cat

The male lion knows its place as ruler of the **pride**. Though outnumbered by lionesses and cubs, it shows its authority with its mane and loud roar. It usually eats first even though the lionesses do the hunting. Life at the top is lonely and scary, however. Another male always seems to have its eyes on the throne!

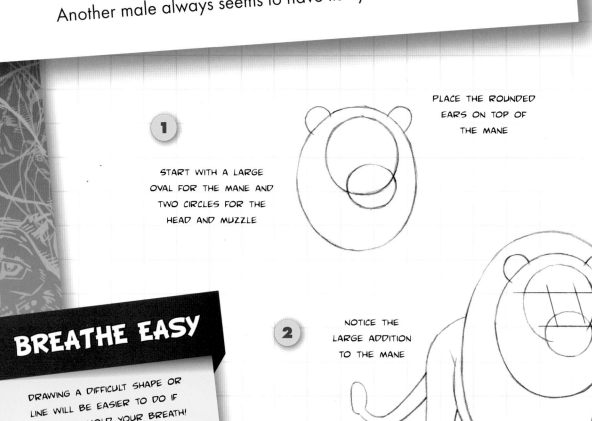

1

START WITH A LARGE OVAL FOR THE MANE AND TWO CIRCLES FOR THE HEAD AND MUZZLE

PLACE THE ROUNDED EARS ON TOP OF THE MANE

2

NOTICE THE LARGE ADDITION TO THE MANE

LIGHTLY DRAW THE OUTLINE OF THE LEGS, BODY, AND TAIL

BREATHE EASY

DRAWING A DIFFICULT SHAPE OR LINE WILL BE EASIER TO DO IF YOU DON'T HOLD YOUR BREATH!

3 ADD DETAILS TO THE FACE AND USE LINES TO DIVIDE THE MANE

DRAW THE LARGE PAWS

4 ADD DETAIL TO THE WAVY MANE

5 INK AND COLOR

MALE LIONS ARE BROWNISH TAN WITH A DARKER BROWN MANE.

Snow Leopard
The Majestic Mystery

A cloud of mystery surrounds the snow leopard. It is hard to track this **endangered** cat in the **remote** areas where it lives. However, it is clear that the snow leopard has no fear of heights. It is most often spotted on cliffs and steep slopes. It braves cold, harsh conditions to climb many of the world's highest peaks.

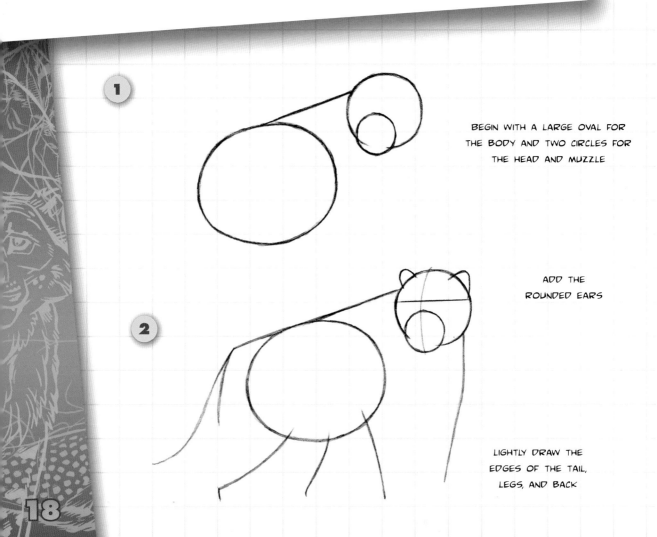

1

BEGIN WITH A LARGE OVAL FOR THE BODY AND TWO CIRCLES FOR THE HEAD AND MUZZLE

ADD THE ROUNDED EARS

2

LIGHTLY DRAW THE EDGES OF THE TAIL, LEGS, AND BACK

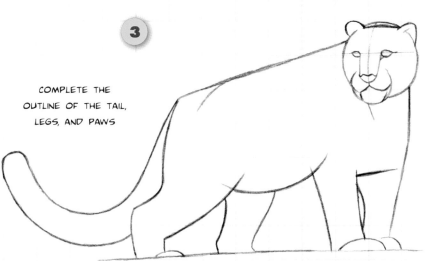

3

COMPLETE THE
OUTLINE OF THE TAIL,
LEGS, AND PAWS

ADD THE EYES, NOSE,
AND MOUTH

4

DRAW THE SPOTS
AND THE LONG FUR ON
THE UNDERSIDE

MIX AND MATCH

YOU CAN MIX COLORS BY GOING
OVER A PREVIOUSLY COLORED
SECTION WITH A NEW COLOR.

5

INK AND COLOR

SNOW LEOPARDS ARE CREAMY
GRAY WITH WHITE UNDERBELLIES
AND BLACK SPOTS.

Tiger
The Largest Cat

The tiger is a sizable foe. Weighing in at more than 700 pounds (318 kilograms), this striped predator is the largest cat. Both animals and people know to keep their distance from this beast. It is one of nature's deadliest animals and is not afraid to make a meal of anything that gets in its way!

KEEP YOUR EDGE!

TO AVOID SHARPENING TOO MUCH, ROTATE YOUR PENCIL SLIGHTLY TO FIND A SHARP EDGE.

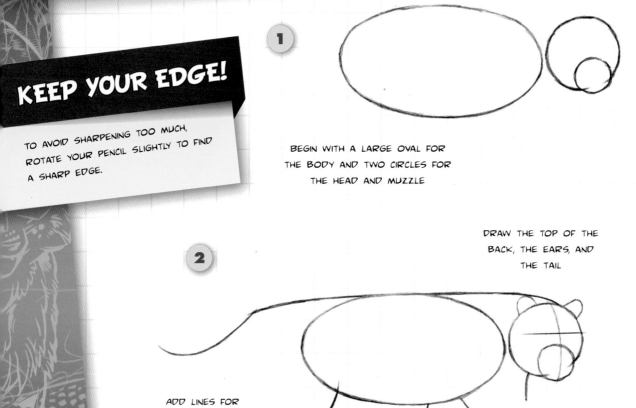

1

BEGIN WITH A LARGE OVAL FOR THE BODY AND TWO CIRCLES FOR THE HEAD AND MUZZLE

2

DRAW THE TOP OF THE BACK, THE EARS, AND THE TAIL

ADD LINES FOR THE LEGS

COMPLETE THE OUTLINE OF THE
TAIL AND LEGS

3

ADD THE EYES
AND NOSE

DRAW THE STRIPES

4

ADD DETAILS
TO THE FACE
AND PAWS

5

INK AND COLOR

MOST TIGERS ARE
ORANGE WITH WHITE
ON THE FACE
AND UNDERSIDE.

GLOSSARY

aliases—alternate names that one goes by

bobbed—very short

camouflage—coloring and patterns that blend in with the surroundings

elusive—difficult to find

endangered—at risk of becoming extinct

feline—relating to cats

pride—a group of lions that live together

remote—far removed from human development

rosettes—the flower-shaped spots on a leopard's coat

suffocate—to keep from breathing

tufts—clumps

TO LEARN MORE

At the Library

Arcturus Publishing. *3-D Thrillers: Big Cats and Ferocious Jungle Animals*. New York, N.Y.: Scholastic, 2010.

Carney, Elizabeth. *National Geographic Kids Everything Big Cats: Pictures to Purr About and Info to Make You Roar!* Washington, D.C.: National Geographic, 2011.

Halpern, Monica. *Big Cats: Drawing and Reading*. Vero Beach, Fla.: Rourke Pub., 2011.

On the Web

Learning more about big cats is as easy as 1, 2, 3.

1. Go to www.factsurfer.com.

2. Enter "big cats" into the search box.

3. Click the "Surf" button and you will see a list of related Web sites.

With factsurfer.com, finding more information is just a click away.

INDEX